Delicate Stars

Elizabeth Schindler

BookLeaf Publishing

India | USA | UK

Presentation by *BookLeaf Publishing*

Web: www.bookleafpub.com

E-mail: info@bookleafpub.com

ISBN: 9789358316902

First edition 2023

To all of the words in all of the languages,
because theirs is an immortal power.

ACKNOWLEDGEMENT

I must begin by thanking my parents. They are the most hard-working, selfless, and loving people I know. Without their support, I would never have ended up where I am today, in every sense of "ending up." From there, I am indebted to the beautiful friends I surround myself with. I am beyond lucky to have such intelligent and caring friends -- it is because of them that I have formed my perspective on life and all of its important facets. I want to also thank the professors in the English Department at the University of Illinois, as every one of them challenged me to craft my writing into a skill I didn't believe I possessed. And finally, I thank my partner, who loves me unconditionally and makes me a better person.

PREFACE

A year is not one body. Its seasons interlace their fingers, but they also walk alone. In my attempt at describing the past year of my life, I walk with the seasons from spring until winter. It is my hope that this collage will bring others solace as we all attempt to unify that which cannot be unified.

breaking out of the cold

there's a birthmark on my butt
in the shape of a cloud
and i used to tell my friends
it meant i was an angel.
now i'd guess it's likely
because my head is
always in the clouds
and the bruises on my knees
would agree with that.

there are two red spots
on the bridge of my nose
where my glasses have clung
for twenty years
claiming my face as their own.
they gave the backs of my ears
extra layers, too
and send a tingle
down my spine
if they're gone for too long.

there are scratches and burns
and scars and creases and
wrinkles and stretch marks
that adorn me,

weaved together in
a quilt of experience.
and the ink patterns i designed
to be cut into my skin
is my complement –
another element of the masterpiece.

march 22

<pre>
            do
          you ever
         go to a café
        and   sit
        way   in
        the   back,
        im-   perc-
       eptible   to
      every-   one   but
      your   smiling   waiter
      and   lower your   volume
      in   your headphones   just
     right   so you can hear   that
     Amy   doesn't like   the
     venue   for the wed-   ding
      and   Jack would   like
       a   London   Fog
      and   Chris   can't
       wait   for
        the   play?
         so deliciously
           inform-
           ative.
</pre>

is it may? oh no it's april

4

you know,

there's nothing quite like the taste
of the sun on the first warm day.

now it's may, and i'm ready

5

can skyscrapers be embarrassed?
today it looked like they were –
magenta hues emblazoned
and reflected back and forth.

like they were constantly
telling the punchline of
an inappropriate joke,
or reciting cyclical compliments.

i got one of those yesterday, too.
a woman on the street told me
i made my dress beautiful –
it's funny how these early
spring days make us all kinder.

walking in june

i put walls around my eyes
so i could see in front of me
better, and what i noticed
was every pair of eyes
wore something different.
blinds half open
to subdue the light;
curtains to hide
behind; nets to catch
unknowing prey;
fences to shut them out.
maybe tomorrow i'll swap
the walls for something else.

it's my birthday

my father likes to remind me
every chance he gets
that i'm "a good person."
is it a mantra?
a suggestion?
an affirmation that
even if he has messed up in life,
at least his child is good?
a ritual,
like holy water,
which he so graciously
doused me in.
i wonder if he's guessed
at how my brain floods
with every shameful thing I've done –
every single thing that i recall
the moment he recites those words.
"thank you, daddy,"
says the pit in my stomach.

july ninth

                    discombobulation
          can be articulated   by getting close
to someone
by the fire that burns
                    lights up your soul
                         your smile
only to fizzle into scorching ash
                         when you remember
it's easier to be alone.
you, who has been hurt,
          you aren't used to the fire
anymore.
                                   and a fire needs
kindling --
doubt   fear   passion   frenzy…
fear.
                                   after it
reignites with these,
          he smiles at you
with that special light
                         and you blow on the
embers
to start another blaze.

the beginning of august

9

it's different because
when we sigh
after making love
i escape reality
and also feel it twice as much

sobbing to the sun

my pages haven't been held
in a while and
the crease in the binding
is much deeper,
but this is how the process goes.
days have felt longer, fuller,
quieter, emptier,
catastrophic,
bitterly beautiful.
mourning in the summer
feels like drowning and
darkness is scarier
days are too long
nights are too quiet.
but at least
i have love, still.

still sobbing, but happier

it makes me want to cry
that we share the same sky
because it could have been
so different – the when,
the where, the how, the why.
why are we so lucky, then
to be congruous best friends?

three different days (august & september)

life is time, which is Change, which is time.
today at the exact same time as someone next to me,
i sat down on the blue subway seat.

"dangerous heat," says my weather app. I stay
home alone with my thoughts, but
at least Alone doesn't taste like a stale chip today.

the close of summer feels soft, sticky, and
sweet. cicada murmurs always envelope me
in Familiarity, and i'm mesmerized by sunsets.

september is in love

can we fill the space
between our fingers
with masking tape and glue
so we never have to be apart?

attach a zipper to our lips
so we can kiss and kiss and kiss
combine our flesh once and for all
then use a needle and thread for our hearts?

it's too cold to swim

complacency latches on
like a leech, a parasite
eating away at resolve;
one week communication's clear,
the next a bit murky,
and so on and
so on
until recognition is
invisible
and the leech can strike.
confidence won't cleanse
the wound, now --
what will come of me?

the second to last day of october

i am many pieces,
many formats, many phases;
a feather drifting on a lake, or
an erupting volcano.
i am many people
who have trained my feet to step
many places, many spaces;
circumnavigation's protégé.
i am dripping with facets,
and never again
will i reduce
to one.

halloween

16

a solitary leaf
charred dark brown
at the edges
is the last one to drop

down

and be engulfed
among its family.
a deep sigh
from the wind
in the bare tree's
branches tells of

death.

35 degrees farenheit

it's in the crevices of mourning
that we find our true pain
when everything blends together
each day grey and all the same

as if it's cloudy when it's not
our skin doesn't feel the heat
and when our eyes slip out of
focus we start tripping in the street

that tunnel they say has a light
at the end of it isn't in sight
and we don't know what's left or right
or if it's better to fly or fight

driving in november

a lonely place
full only of unspoken memories
sits in the dust by route 66.
the O and L on its sign
flicker in muted pink,
and there's vacancy tonight.

winter weekend

19

saturday, crimson. / we're holding hands on the
table. / chatter abounds but i don't hear a sound,
because / our little space is much louder. / i
smile into my drink as you say, / "i never really
believed them when they told me 'when you
know, you know…' / but now i do. i really do." /
i want to cry and shout and marry you. / instead i
squeeze your hand. / and we continue to bask in
the warmth of our little space / until we go back
downstairs to meet our friends. /

december 1

20

in your warmth i thawed
but ice forms quickly, creeping –
is this flame weaker?

staying home

21

there my heater goes
click whoosh tack tack
creeeeeeek
almost rhythmic to my
heart's beat
while i lay in bed
thinking.

happy new year

my favorite is when we dance
not around each other's questions
but perfectly in time.

when we lean forward for a laugh
with floating friends, finding our feet
or tap our toes while doing dishes
to the beat of tuesday night.

let's not tiptoe past the sad songs
let's jive, let's groove, let's move
let's pirouette at 3 a.m.
or salsa at noon.

my favorite is this, the dance
through unchoreographed moments
let's step forward for the next.

9 789358 316902